PERSO[NAL]

M000121755

Name:

Address:

Telephone: Email:

Employer:

Address:

Telephone: Email:

MEDICAL INFORMATION

Physician: Telephone:

Allergies:

Medications:

Blood Type:

Insurer:

IN CASE OF EMERGENCY, NOTIFY

Name:

Address:

Telephone: Relationship:

© 2021 by Barbour Publishing, Inc.

ISBN 978-1-64352-917-2

Published by Barbour Publishing, Inc., 1810 Barbour Drive, Uhrichsville, Ohio 44683, www.barbourbooks.com

Our mission is to inspire the world with the life-changing message of the Bible.

Member of the
Evangelical Christian
Publishers Association

Printed in China.

Choose
PRAYER

· 2022 PLANNER ·

DAYMAKER
A Division of Barbour Publishing

Introduction

It's easy to get bogged down in the responsibilities, to-do lists, and schedules of everyday life. But God gives us each day to live and thrive in His presence—to *choose prayer* because He cares about everything we have to say.

Take time from your busy life to take delight in every prayer-filled moment. This planner is a good way to start. Use it to assist in the organization of the daily grind, and allow the readings and scripture to bless your heart all 365 days of 2022.

2022

JANUARY

S	M	T	W	T	F	S
						1
2	3	4	5	6	7	8
9	10	11	12	13	14	15
16	17	18	19	20	21	22
23	24	25	26	27	28	29
30	31					

FEBRUARY

S	M	T	W	T	F	S
		1	2	3	4	5
6	7	8	9	10	11	12
13	14	15	16	17	18	19
20	21	22	23	24	25	26
27	28					

MAY

S	M	T	W	T	F	S
1	2	3	4	5	6	7
8	9	10	11	12	13	14
15	16	17	18	19	20	21
22	23	24	25	26	27	28
29	30	31				

JUNE

S	M	T	W	T	F	S
			1	2	3	4
5	6	7	8	9	10	11
12	13	14	15	16	17	18
19	20	21	22	23	24	25
26	27	28	29	30		

SEPTEMBER

S	M	T	W	T	F	S
				1	2	3
4	5	6	7	8	9	10
11	12	13	14	15	16	17
18	19	20	21	22	23	24
25	26	27	28	29	30	

OCTOBER

S	M	T	W	T	F	S
						1
2	3	4	5	6	7	8
9	10	11	12	13	14	15
16	17	18	19	20	21	22
23	24	25	26	27	28	29
30	31					

YEAR–AT–A–GLANCE

MARCH

S	M	T	W	T	F	S
		1	2	3	4	5
6	7	8	9	10	11	12
13	14	15	16	17	18	19
20	21	22	23	24	25	26
27	28	29	30	31		

APRIL

S	M	T	W	T	F	S
					1	2
3	4	5	6	7	8	9
10	11	12	13	14	15	16
17	18	19	20	21	22	23
24	25	26	27	28	29	30

JULY

S	M	T	W	T	F	S
					1	2
3	4	5	6	7	8	9
10	11	12	13	14	15	16
17	18	19	20	21	22	23
24	25	26	27	28	29	30
31						

AUGUST

S	M	T	W	T	F	S
	1	2	3	4	5	6
7	8	9	10	11	12	13
14	15	16	17	18	19	20
21	22	23	24	25	26	27
28	29	30	31			

NOVEMBER

S	M	T	W	T	F	S
		1	2	3	4	5
6	7	8	9	10	11	12
13	14	15	16	17	18	19
20	21	22	23	24	25	26
27	28	29	30			

DECEMBER

S	M	T	W	T	F	S
				1	2	3
4	5	6	7	8	9	10
11	12	13	14	15	16	17
18	19	20	21	22	23	24
25	26	27	28	29	30	31

AUGUST *2021*

SUNDAY	MONDAY	TUESDAY	WEDNESDAY
1	2	3	4
8	9	10	11
15	16	17	18
22	23	24	25
29	30	31	1

THURSDAY	FRIDAY	SATURDAY
5	6	7
12	13	14
19	20	21
26	27	28
2	3	4

JULY

S	M	T	W	T	F	S
					1	2	3
4	5	6	7	8	9	10
11	12	13	14	15	16	17
18	19	20	21	22	23	24
25	26	27	28	29	30	31

SEPTEMBER

S	M	T	W	T	F	S
			1	2	3	4
5	6	7	8	9	10	11
12	13	14	15	16	17	18
19	20	21	22	23	24	25
26	27	28	29	30		

PRAYERFUL
CONSIDERATION

Have you ever had to make a decision but didn't know what to do? As Christians, we have a reliable resource for counsel. When decision-making poses a threat to our serenity and peace, Proverbs 3:5–6 provides sound advice.

God provides the solution to decision-making with a promise—namely, if we take all our concerns to God, He will direct our paths. When we're tempted to act on our own wisdom, the Lord tells us to stop, reflect, and prayerfully consider each matter. He gives us uncomplicated advice for our major and not-so-major decisions. The question is, will we listen? That's the most important decision of all.

---

*Often, Lord, I run on ahead of You and make
decisions on my own. Help me to remember
that even with small decisions I need
to seek Your will. Amen.*

Goals FOR THE *Month*

_____

_____

_____

_____

_____

_____

_____

_____

_____

_____

_____

_____

_____

_____

_____

_____

Trust in the LORD with all your heart
and lean not on your own understanding;
in all your ways submit to him, and he
will make your paths straight.
PROVERBS 3:5–6 NIV

God listens to us when we pray. He hears every word and is compassionate. All we have to do is share our concerns with Him and wait faithfully for what He will provide.

SUNDAY, AUGUST 1

MONDAY, AUGUST 2

TUESDAY, AUGUST 3

WEDNESDAY, AUGUST 4

THURSDAY, AUGUST 5

FRIDAY, AUGUST 6

SATURDAY, AUGUST 7

Never stop praying.
1 THESSALONIANS 5:17 NLT

When we learn to trust that God can protect us and work out our problems, then we can lie down peacefully and sleep (Psalm 4:8). That same trust gives us the strength to face our days with confidence.

SUNDAY, AUGUST 8

MONDAY, AUGUST 9

TUESDAY, AUGUST 10

WEDNESDAY, AUGUST 11

THURSDAY, AUGUST 12

FRIDAY, AUGUST 13

SATURDAY, AUGUST 14

Be still,
and know that I am God.
PSALM 46:10 NKJV

We bring absolutely nothing to God. But in God's great mercy, He chooses to hear, love, and forgive us.

SUNDAY, AUGUST 15

MONDAY, AUGUST 16

TUESDAY, AUGUST 17

WEDNESDAY, AUGUST 18

THURSDAY, AUGUST 19

FRIDAY, AUGUST 20

SATURDAY, AUGUST 21

*"We do not make requests of
you because we are righteous,
but because of your great mercy."*
DANIEL 9:18 NIV

God knows our needs even before we give voice to them in prayer. We can rest in the knowledge that even before the words leave our lips, God has already heard them, and He has already answered them.

SUNDAY, AUGUST 22

MONDAY, AUGUST 23

TUESDAY, AUGUST 24

WEDNESDAY, AUGUST 25

THURSDAY, AUGUST 26

FRIDAY, AUGUST 27

SATURDAY, AUGUST 28

"As soon as you began to pray, a word went out, which I have come to tell you, for you are highly esteemed."

DANIEL 9:23 NIV

SEPTEMBER *2021*

SUNDAY	MONDAY	TUESDAY	WEDNESDAY
29	30	31	1
5	6 *Labor Day*	7	8
12	13	14	15
19	20	21	22 *First Day of Autumn*
26	27	28	29

THURSDAY	FRIDAY	SATURDAY
2	3	4
9	10	11
16	17	18
23	24	25
30	1	2

AUGUST

S	M	T	W	T	F	S
1	2	3	4	5	6	7
8	9	10	11	12	13	14
15	16	17	18	19	20	21
22	23	24	25	26	27	28
29	30	31				

OCTOBER

S	M	T	W	T	F	S
					1	2
3	4	5	6	7	8	9
10	11	12	13	14	15	16
17	18	19	20	21	22	23
24	25	26	27	28	29	30
31						

BE ANXIOUS
FOR NOTHING

"Be anxious for nothing" sounds like great advice, but at times most of us have the feeling that it only works for highly mature saints and is not practical for the average Christian.

Yet the key to making it work is found in the same verse: we can "be anxious for nothing" if we are continually taking those problems to God in prayer, thanking Him for solving past problems, and trusting Him to work the current situation out. Praying about things, of course, shouldn't keep us from doing what God inspires us to do to solve the problems. But we should trust and pray instead of fretting and worrying.

Father, anxiety makes me weary. Today I ask You to take all my problems and work them out for my good. Show me the way, Lord, and I will obey You. Amen.

Goals FOR THE *Month*

---

*Be anxious for nothing, but in everything by
prayer and supplication, with thanksgiving,
let your requests be made known to God.*

PHILIPPIANS 4:6 NKJV

The actions of our hearts speak louder than our words. And if our worship consists of mindlessly repeating words and going with the flow, we are missing out on connecting with a God who fiercely loves us and desires to be in an unscripted relationship with us.

SUNDAY, AUGUST 29

MONDAY, AUGUST 30

TUESDAY, AUGUST 31

WEDNESDAY, SEPTEMBER 1

THURSDAY, SEPTEMBER 2

FRIDAY, SEPTEMBER 3

SATURDAY, SEPTEMBER 4

*And so the Lord says, "These people say they are mine.
They honor me with their lips, but their hearts are far
from me. And their worship of me is nothing
but man-made rules learned by rote."*

ISAIAH 29:13 NLT

When you're praying for wisdom in a complex or desperate situation, fix this thought firmly in your mind: You may have no clue as to the right answer, but God certainly does! His understanding is without end.

SUNDAY, SEPTEMBER 5

MONDAY, SEPTEMBER 6 *Labor Day*

TUESDAY, SEPTEMBER 7

WEDNESDAY, SEPTEMBER 8

THURSDAY, SEPTEMBER 9

FRIDAY, SEPTEMBER 10

SATURDAY, SEPTEMBER 11

Great is our Lord, and of great power:
his understanding is infinite.
PSALM 147:5 KJV

God wanted to hear prayers of repentance, and He wanted that repentance to be followed by action. He commanded, "Cease to do evil, learn to do good" (Isaiah 1:16–17 RSV).

SUNDAY, SEPTEMBER 12

MONDAY, SEPTEMBER 13

TUESDAY, SEPTEMBER 14

WEDNESDAY, SEPTEMBER 15

THURSDAY, SEPTEMBER 16

FRIDAY, SEPTEMBER 17

SATURDAY, SEPTEMBER 18

*"Come now, let us reason together, says the
LORD: though your sins are like scarlet, they shall
be as white as snow; though they are red like
crimson, they shall become like wool."*

ISAIAH 1:18 RSV

We must be honest about our faith, praying for God to strengthen it. Only then can God truly begin the healing process.

SUNDAY, SEPTEMBER 19

MONDAY, SEPTEMBER 20

TUESDAY, SEPTEMBER 21

WEDNESDAY, SEPTEMBER 22   *First Day of Autumn*

THURSDAY, SEPTEMBER 23

FRIDAY, SEPTEMBER 24

SATURDAY, SEPTEMBER 25

*"I do believe;
help me overcome my unbelief!"*
MARK 9:24 NIV

No matter how distant God may seem, we need to keep talking to Him. Keep praying. Keep pouring out our hearts. We can know that God will answer in His time.

SUNDAY, SEPTEMBER 26

MONDAY, SEPTEMBER 27

TUESDAY, SEPTEMBER 28

WEDNESDAY, SEPTEMBER 29

THURSDAY, SEPTEMBER 30

FRIDAY, OCTOBER 1

SATURDAY, OCTOBER 2

Answer me when I call to you, my righteous
God. Give me relief from my distress;
have mercy on me and hear my prayer.

PSALM 4:1 NIV

OCTOBER *2021*

SUNDAY	MONDAY	TUESDAY	WEDNESDAY
26	27	28	29
3	4	5	6
10	11	12	13
	Columbus Day		
17	18	19	20
24	25	26	27
Halloween 31			

THURSDAY	FRIDAY	SATURDAY
30	1	2
7	8	9
14	15	16
21	22	23
28	29	30

SEPTEMBER

S	M	T	W	T	F	S
			1	2	3	4
5	6	7	8	9	10	11
12	13	14	15	16	17	18
19	20	21	22	23	24	25
26	27	28	29	30		

NOVEMBER

S	M	T	W	T	F	S
	1	2	3	4	5	6
7	8	9	10	11	12	13
14	15	16	17	18	19	20
21	22	23	24	25	26	27
28	29	30				

WHEN WORDS FAIL ME

Sometimes Christians feel so overwhelmed by their needs or by the greatness of God that they simply can't pray. When the words won't come, God helps to create them. Paul says in Romans 8:26 (NLT), "And the Holy Spirit helps us in our weakness. For example, we don't know what God wants us to pray for. But the Holy Spirit prays for us with groanings that cannot be expressed in words."

God hears your prayers even before you pray them. When you don't know what to say and the words won't come, you can simply ask God to help you by praying on your behalf.

Dear God, I'm grateful today that
in my silence You still hear me. Amen.

Goals FOR THE *Month*

Before a word is on my tongue you,
LORD, know it completely.
PSALM 139:4 NIV

Having fellowship with God is talking to our best Friend, knowing He understands and provides help and wisdom along life's journey. It's demonstrating our faith and trust in the One who knows us better than anyone.

SUNDAY, OCTOBER 3

MONDAY, OCTOBER 4

TUESDAY, OCTOBER 5

WEDNESDAY, OCTOBER 6

THURSDAY, OCTOBER 7

FRIDAY, OCTOBER 8

SATURDAY, OCTOBER 9

*God is faithful, who has called you into fellowship
with his Son, Jesus Christ our Lord.*
1 CORINTHIANS 1:9 NIV

While God doesn't always choose to fix things with a snap of His fingers, we can be assured that He will see us through to the other side of our troubles by a smoother path than we'd travel without Him. He's waiting to help us. All we have to do is call.

SUNDAY, OCTOBER 10

MONDAY, OCTOBER 11   *Columbus Day*

TUESDAY, OCTOBER 12

WEDNESDAY, OCTOBER 13

THURSDAY, OCTOBER 14

FRIDAY, OCTOBER 15

SATURDAY, OCTOBER 16

"Call on me in the day of trouble;
I will deliver you, and you will honor me."
PSALM 50:15 NIV

When Christians pray, it shows not only their faith in God but also their trust in His faithfulness toward them. In His time, the Lord will come and bring justice to His people.

SUNDAY, OCTOBER 17

MONDAY, OCTOBER 18

TUESDAY, OCTOBER 19

WEDNESDAY, OCTOBER 20

THURSDAY, OCTOBER 21

FRIDAY, OCTOBER 22

SATURDAY, OCTOBER 23

*Rejoice always, pray continually, give thanks
in all circumstances; for this is God's
will for you in Christ Jesus.*
1 THESSALONIANS 5:16–18 NIV

When you begin to worry that you don't have what it takes to meet life's demands, remember that you don't have to—because God does.

SUNDAY, OCTOBER 24

MONDAY, OCTOBER 25

TUESDAY, OCTOBER 26

WEDNESDAY, OCTOBER 27

THURSDAY, OCTOBER 28

FRIDAY, OCTOBER 29

SATURDAY, OCTOBER 30

*"Pray that the LORD your God will show
us what to do and where to go."*

JEREMIAH 42:3 NLT

NOVEMBER *2021*

SUNDAY	MONDAY	TUESDAY	WEDNESDAY
31	1	2 *Election Day*	3
7 *Daylight Saving Time Ends*	8	9	10
14	15	16	17
21	22	23	24
28 *Hanukkah Begins at Sundown*	29	30	1

THURSDAY	FRIDAY	SATURDAY
4	5	6
11	12	13
Veterans Day		
18	19	20
25	26	27
Thanksgiving Day		
2	3	4

OCTOBER

S	M	T	W	T	F	S
					1	2
3	4	5	6	7	8	9
10	11	12	13	14	15	16
17	18	19	20	21	22	23
24	25	26	27	28	29	30
31						

DECEMBER

S	M	T	W	T	F	S
			1	2	3	4
5	6	7	8	9	10	11
12	13	14	15	16	17	18
19	20	21	22	23	24	25
26	27	28	29	30	31	

NOV

WHEN GOD'S
PEOPLE PRAY

God, in all His power, has invited us to come alongside Him. He's asked us to join Him in His work by praying for each other.

For centuries, God's people have been treated unfairly and unjustly. Yet we've survived, when other groups haven't. The reason we've survived when so many have sought to silence us is because we have something our enemies don't have. We have the power of God within us.

When we pray, we call upon every resource available to us as the children of God. We call upon God's strength, His compassion, His ferocity, His mercy, His love, and His justice. We have the ability to extend God's reach to the other side of our town or the other side of the world, all because we pray.

Dear Father, thank You for letting me join You in Your work. Please bless the people who love You, wherever they are in this world. Allow them to prosper according to their love for You. Amen.

Goals FOR THE *Month*

Pray for the peace of Jerusalem:
"May those who love you be secure."

PSALM 122:6 NIV

God is looking for ordinary men and women whose prayers reflect hearts completely committed to Him.

SUNDAY, OCTOBER 31   *Halloween*

MONDAY, NOVEMBER 1

TUESDAY, NOVEMBER 2   *Election Day*

WEDNESDAY, NOVEMBER 3

THURSDAY, NOVEMBER 4

FRIDAY, NOVEMBER 5

SATURDAY, NOVEMBER 6

*"The eyes of the LORD search the whole
earth in order to strengthen those whose
hearts are fully committed to him."*
2 CHRONICLES 16:9 NLT

NOVEMBER 2021

When we feel far from God, sometimes the last thing we want to do is talk to Him. But it is through honest, heartfelt conversation, however one-sided it may seem to us, that we draw into God's presence. When we feel far from God, we need to keep talking. He's there.

SUNDAY, NOVEMBER 7 *Daylight Saving Time Ends*

MONDAY, NOVEMBER 8

TUESDAY, NOVEMBER 9

WEDNESDAY, NOVEMBER 10

THURSDAY, NOVEMBER 11   *Veterans Day*

FRIDAY, NOVEMBER 12

SATURDAY, NOVEMBER 13

*The LORD is near to all who call on him,
to all who call on him in truth.*
PSALM 145:18 NIV

Maybe your quiet place is your garden or the beach. Wherever it is, enjoy some time alone with God. Draw near to Him in prayer, and He will draw near to you.

SUNDAY, NOVEMBER 14

MONDAY, NOVEMBER 15

TUESDAY, NOVEMBER 16

WEDNESDAY, NOVEMBER 17

THURSDAY, NOVEMBER 18

FRIDAY, NOVEMBER 19

SATURDAY, NOVEMBER 20

Come near to God and he
will come near to you.
JAMES 4:8 NIV

NOVEMBER 2021

You are not alone. Christ sent a Comforter, a Counselor, the Holy Ghost, the Spirit of Truth. When you don't know what to pray, the Bible promises that the Spirit has you covered.

SUNDAY, NOVEMBER 21

MONDAY, NOVEMBER 22

TUESDAY, NOVEMBER 23

WEDNESDAY, NOVEMBER 24

THURSDAY, NOVEMBER 25   *Thanksgiving Day*

FRIDAY, NOVEMBER 26

SATURDAY, NOVEMBER 27

And the Holy Spirit helps us in our weakness.
For example, we don't know what God wants us
to pray for. But the Holy Spirit prays for us with
groanings that cannot be expressed in words.
ROMANS 8:26 NLT

DECEMBER *2021*

SUNDAY	MONDAY	TUESDAY	WEDNESDAY
28	29	30	1
5	6	7	8
12	13	14	15
19	20	21 *First Day of Winter*	22
26	27	28	29

THURSDAY	FRIDAY	SATURDAY
2	3	4
9	10	11
16	17	18
23	24 *Christmas Eve*	25 *Christmas Day*
30	31 *New Year's Eve*	1

NOVEMBER

S	M	T	W	T	F	S
	1	2	3	4	5	6
7	8	9	10	11	12	13
14	15	16	17	18	19	20
21	22	23	24	25	26	27
28	29	30				

JANUARY

S	M	T	W	T	F	S
						1
2	3	4	5	6	7	8
9	10	11	12	13	14	15
16	17	18	19	20	21	22
23	24	25	26	27	28	29
30	31					

DEC

JUST IN TIME

As believers, our lives become exciting when we wait on God to direct our paths, because He knows what is best for us at any given moment. His plans and agenda are never wrong.

Once we fully realize He knows best and turn our lives over to the Spirit for direction, we can allow God to be in charge of our calendar; His timing is what is paramount.

When chomping at the bit for a job offer or for a proposal, His timing might seem slow. "Hurry up, God!" we groan. But when we learn to patiently wait on His promises, we will see that the plans He has for us are more than we dared hope for—or dreamed of. God promises to answer us; and He never fails to be right on time.

Lord, I want Your perfect will in my life.
Help me learn to wait upon You. Amen.

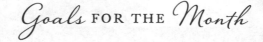

Goals FOR THE Month

---

*Therefore let us [with privilege] approach the
throne of grace [that is, the throne of God's
gracious favor] with confidence and without
fear, so that we may receive mercy [for our
failures] and find [His amazing] grace to help
in time of need [an appropriate blessing,
coming just at the right moment].*

HEBREWS 4:16 AMP

Tell God what you need and thank Him in advance for what He will do. God will always provide. He will always show up. He does not want you to worry.

SUNDAY, NOVEMBER 28 *Hanukkah Begins at Sundown*

MONDAY, NOVEMBER 29

TUESDAY, NOVEMBER 30

WEDNESDAY, DECEMBER 1

THURSDAY, DECEMBER 2

FRIDAY, DECEMBER 3

SATURDAY, DECEMBER 4

*Don't worry about anything; instead,
pray about everything. Tell God what you
need, and thank him for all he has done.*

PHILIPPIANS 4:6 NLT

When we pray for others, we ask God to intervene and to make Himself known to them. We can pray for God's plan and purpose in their lives. We can ask God to bless them or protect them.

SUNDAY, DECEMBER 5

MONDAY, DECEMBER 6

TUESDAY, DECEMBER 7

WEDNESDAY, DECEMBER 8

THURSDAY, DECEMBER 9

FRIDAY, DECEMBER 10

SATURDAY, DECEMBER 11

First of all, then, I urge that petitions (specific
requests), prayers, intercessions (prayers for others) and
thanksgivings be offered on behalf of all people. . . .
This [kind of praying] is good and acceptable and
pleasing in the sight of God our Savior.
1 TIMOTHY 2:1, 3 AMP

We are so blessed to have been given the Holy Spirit within to keep us in tune with God's will. Through His guidance, that still, small voice, we can rest assured our priorities will stay focused on Jesus.

SUNDAY, DECEMBER 12

MONDAY, DECEMBER 13

TUESDAY, DECEMBER 14

WEDNESDAY, DECEMBER 15

THURSDAY, DECEMBER 16

FRIDAY, DECEMBER 17

SATURDAY, DECEMBER 18

*I have fought a good fight, I have finished
my course, I have kept the faith.*
2 TIMOTHY 4:7 KJV

DECEMBER *2021*

When we offer to pray for someone, we can say it with the confidence that our prayers will be heard. They will be answered. And they will make a beautiful difference in the lives of those for whom we pray.

SUNDAY, DECEMBER 19

MONDAY, DECEMBER 20

TUESDAY, DECEMBER 21 *First Day of Winter*

WEDNESDAY, DECEMBER 22

THURSDAY, DECEMBER 23

FRIDAY, DECEMBER 24   *Christmas Eve*

SATURDAY, DECEMBER 25   *Christmas Day*

*You help us by your prayers. Then many will
give thanks on our behalf for the gracious favor
granted us in answer to the prayers of many.*

2 CORINTHIANS 1:11 NIV

God wants to travel the journey with us. He's a wonderful Companion, offering wisdom and comfort for every aspect of our lives. But He can only do that if we let Him into our schedules, every minute of every day.

___

SUNDAY, DECEMBER 26

___

MONDAY, DECEMBER 27

___

TUESDAY, DECEMBER 28

___

WEDNESDAY, DECEMBER 29

THURSDAY, DECEMBER 30

FRIDAY, DECEMBER 31   *New Year's Eve*

SATURDAY, JANUARY 1   *New Year's Day*

Pray in the Spirit at all times
with all kinds of prayers.
EPHESIANS 6:18 NCV

JANUARY *2022*

SUNDAY	MONDAY	TUESDAY	WEDNESDAY
26	27	28	29
2	3	4	5
9	10	11	12
16	17 *Martin Luther King Jr. Day*	18	19
23 / 30	24 / 31	25	26

THURSDAY	FRIDAY	SATURDAY
30	31	1 *New Year's Day*
6	7	8
13	14	15
20	21	22
27	28	29

DECEMBER

S	M	T	W	T	F	S
			1	2	3	4
5	6	7	8	9	10	11
12	13	14	15	16	17	18
19	20	21	22	23	24	25
26	27	28	29	30	31	

FEBRUARY

S	M	T	W	T	F	S
		1	2	3	4	5
6	7	8	9	10	11	12
13	14	15	16	17	18	19
20	21	22	23	24	25	26
27	28					

BEFORE YOU ASK

In the Lord's Prayer, Jesus teaches His followers how to pray. He begins, "Our Father in heaven, may your name be kept holy. May your kingdom come soon. May your will be done on earth, as it is in heaven" (Matthew 6:9–10 NLT). First, Jesus honors God's holiness. Next, He shows faith in God's promise of reigning over the earth and redeeming His people. Then He accepts God's perfect will. Praise, faith, and acceptance come before asking. Jesus reminds believers to honor God first, put God's will second, and pray for their own needs third. His prayer begins with God and ends with Him: "For thine is the kingdom, and the power, and the glory, for ever. Amen" (Matthew 6:13 KJV).

Bring your requests to God. Ask specifically and confidently, but remember Jesus' model—put God first in your prayers.

Dear God, I praise You. My faith rests in You, and I accept whatever Your will is for my life. Amen.

Goals FOR THE *Month*

---

*"Seek the Kingdom of God above all else,
and live righteously, and he will give
you everything you need."*

MATTHEW 6:33 NLT

When we don't get the answers we want from God, it's okay to feel disappointed. He understands. But we must never doubt His goodness or His motives. We must stand firm in our belief that God's love for us will never change.

SUNDAY, JANUARY 2

MONDAY, JANUARY 3

TUESDAY, JANUARY 4

WEDNESDAY, JANUARY 5

THURSDAY, JANUARY 6

FRIDAY, JANUARY 7

SATURDAY, JANUARY 8

But when you ask God, you must believe and not doubt. Anyone who doubts is like a wave in the sea, blown up and down by the wind.

JAMES 1:6 NCV

If we want our prayers to hold extra power, we need to live righteously. When we have God's approval on our lives, we can also know we have God's ear about all sorts of things. When we walk in God's will, we have access to God's power.

SUNDAY, JANUARY 9

....

....

....

MONDAY, JANUARY 10

....

....

....

TUESDAY, JANUARY 11

....

....

....

WEDNESDAY, JANUARY 12

THURSDAY, JANUARY 13

FRIDAY, JANUARY 14

SATURDAY, JANUARY 15

Therefore confess your sins to each other and pray for each other so that you may be healed. The prayer of a righteous person is powerful and effective.

JAMES 5:16 NIV

Like so many foods that are good for us, all it requires is that first taste, a tiny morsel, which whets the appetite for more of God. Then you can be open to all the goodness, all the fullness of the Lord.

SUNDAY, JANUARY 16

MONDAY, JANUARY 17   *Martin Luther King Jr. Day*

TUESDAY, JANUARY 18

WEDNESDAY, JANUARY 19

THURSDAY, JANUARY 20

FRIDAY, JANUARY 21

SATURDAY, JANUARY 22

*Taste and see that the LORD is good; blessed
is the one who takes refuge in him.*
PSALM 34:8 NIV

God wants a constant relationship with you, and He is available and waiting to do life with you twenty-four hours a day.

SUNDAY, JANUARY 23

MONDAY, JANUARY 24

TUESDAY, JANUARY 25

WEDNESDAY, JANUARY 26

THURSDAY, JANUARY 27

FRIDAY, JANUARY 28

SATURDAY, JANUARY 29

In the morning, LORD, you hear my voice;
in the morning I lay my requests before
you and wait expectantly.
PSALM 5:3 NIV

FEBRUARY 2022

SUNDAY	MONDAY	TUESDAY	WEDNESDAY
30	31	1	2
6	7	8	9
13	14 *Valentine's Day*	15	16
20	21 *Presidents' Day*	22	23
27	28	1	2

THURSDAY	FRIDAY	SATURDAY
3	4	5
10	11	12
17	18	19
24	25	26
3	4	5

JANUARY

S	M	T	W	T	F	S
						1
2	3	4	5	6	7	8
9	10	11	12	13	14	15
16	17	18	19	20	21	22
23	24	25	26	27	28	29
30	31					

MARCH

S	M	T	W	T	F	S
		1	2	3	4	5
6	7	8	9	10	11	12
13	14	15	16	17	18	19
20	21	22	23	24	25	26
27	28	29	30	31		

OUR PRAYER CALLING

Have you ever felt useless to the kingdom of God? Do you think you have little to offer, so you offer little? Consider the eighty-four-year-old widow Anna. She stayed at the temple, worshipping God through prayer and fasting. That was her calling, and she was committed to prayer until the Lord ushered her home.

We need not pray and fast like this dedicated woman did. (In fact, for health reasons, fasting is not always an option.) Yet we are all called to pray. We can pray right where we are, regardless of our age, circumstances, or surroundings. Like Anna, it's our calling.

Lord, please remind me of the calling of prayer on my life, despite my circumstances. Amen.

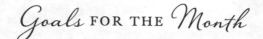

Goals FOR THE *Month*

----

*Then [Anna] lived as a widow to the
age of eighty-four. She never left the
Temple but stayed there day and night,
worshiping God with fasting and prayer.*

LUKE 2:37 NLT

One of the greatest things about the Holy Spirit is that He helps us to distinguish God's call on our lives from the other voices of the world. Pray that God will reveal His good and perfect will for your life.

SUNDAY, JANUARY 30

MONDAY, JANUARY 31

TUESDAY, FEBRUARY 1

WEDNESDAY, FEBRUARY 2

THURSDAY, FEBRUARY 3

FRIDAY, FEBRUARY 4

SATURDAY, FEBRUARY 5

*We have not stopped praying for you. We continually
ask God to fill you with the knowledge of his will
through all the wisdom and understanding
that the Spirit gives.*

COLOSSIANS 1:9 NIV

If only we'd slow down and let the heavenly Father's words sink into our spirits, what a difference we might see in our prayer lives. This day, stop. Listen. See what God has in store for you.

SUNDAY, FEBRUARY 6

MONDAY, FEBRUARY 7

TUESDAY, FEBRUARY 8

WEDNESDAY, FEBRUARY 9

THURSDAY, FEBRUARY 10

FRIDAY, FEBRUARY 11

SATURDAY, FEBRUARY 12

I will listen to what God the LORD says.
PSALM 85:8 NIV

Through prayer we draw near to God and get to know Him better. In doing that, we'll become the thankful, trusting, and faithful children He desires.

SUNDAY, FEBRUARY 13

MONDAY, FEBRUARY 14   *Valentine's Day*

TUESDAY, FEBRUARY 15

WEDNESDAY, FEBRUARY 16

THURSDAY, FEBRUARY 17

FRIDAY, FEBRUARY 18

SATURDAY, FEBRUARY 19

"Sacrifice thank offerings to God, fulfill your vows to the Most High, and call on me in the day of trouble; I will deliver you, and you will honor me."

PSALM 50:14–15 NIV

Adult prayers don't have to be well ordered and formal. God loves hearing His children's voices, and no detail is too little or dull to pray about.

SUNDAY, FEBRUARY 20

MONDAY, FEBRUARY 21 *Presidents' Day*

TUESDAY, FEBRUARY 22

WEDNESDAY, FEBRUARY 23

THURSDAY, FEBRUARY 24

FRIDAY, FEBRUARY 25

SATURDAY, FEBRUARY 26

The LORD directs the steps of the godly.
He delights in every detail of their lives.
PSALM 37:23 NLT

MARCH 2022

SUNDAY	MONDAY	TUESDAY	WEDNESDAY
27	28	1	2 *Ash Wednesday*
6	7	8	9
13 *Daylight Saving Time Begins*	14	15	16
20 *First Day of Spring*	21	22	23
27	28	29	30

THURSDAY	FRIDAY	SATURDAY
3	4	5
10	11	12
17	18	19
St. Patrick's Day		
24	25	26
31	1	2

FEBRUARY

S	M	T	W	T	F	S
		1	2	3	4	5
6	7	8	9	10	11	12
13	14	15	16	17	18	19
20	21	22	23	24	25	26
27	28					

APRIL

S	M	T	W	T	F	S
					1	2
3	4	5	6	7	8	9
10	11	12	13	14	15	16
17	18	19	20	21	22	23
24	25	26	27	28	29	30

HE CARES FOR YOU

Often we feel deserted, as though God doesn't hear our prayers, and we wait. When Moses led the children of Israel out of Egypt toward the promised land, God directed him to go the long way, lest the people turn back quickly when things became difficult. The people placed their hope in an almighty God and followed His lead. When they thirsted, God gave water. When they hungered, He sent manna. No need was unmet.

If God can do this for so many, you can rest assured that He will care for you. He knows your needs before you even ask. Place your hope and trust in Him. He is able. He's proven Himself over and over. Read the scriptures and pray to the One who loves you. His care is infinite—and He will never disappoint you.

Heavenly Father, I know You love me and hear me. I bless Your holy name. Amen.

Goals FOR THE Month

....
....
....
....
....
....
....
....
....
....
....
....
....
....
....

*"You have seen what I did to the Egyptians,
and how I carried you on eagles' wings,
and brought you to Myself."*

EXODUS 19:4 AMP

When you pray, call out to God with your whole heart. Prayer must be more than an afterthought to close each day, as eyelids grow heavy and sleep wins the battle. Seek God. Crave and require His face. Turn toward Him.

SUNDAY, FEBRUARY 27

MONDAY, FEBRUARY 28

TUESDAY, MARCH 1

WEDNESDAY, MARCH 2   *Ash Wednesday*

THURSDAY, MARCH 3

FRIDAY, MARCH 4

SATURDAY, MARCH 5

*"[If] My people, who are called by My Name,
humble themselves, and pray and seek (crave,
require as a necessity) My face and turn from their
wicked ways, then I will hear [them] from heaven,
and forgive their sin and heal their land."*

2 CHRONICLES 7:14 AMP

Whether we like the person who is in office or not, God commands us to pray for those He placed in authority over us. As issues concerning Christ followers emerge, we are called to pray for all people, including those with whom we don't see eye to eye politically.

SUNDAY, MARCH 6

MONDAY, MARCH 7

TUESDAY, MARCH 8

WEDNESDAY, MARCH 9

THURSDAY, MARCH 10

FRIDAY, MARCH 11

SATURDAY, MARCH 12

*I urge, then, first of all, that petitions, prayers,
intercession and thanksgiving be made for all people—
for kings and all those in authority, that we may live
peaceful and quiet lives in all godliness and holiness.*
1 TIMOTHY 2:1–2 NIV

When you lift your requests to the Sovereign God, rest assured that He is ready to answer. Wait expectantly!

SUNDAY, MARCH 13 *Daylight Saving Time Begins*

MONDAY, MARCH 14

TUESDAY, MARCH 15

WEDNESDAY, MARCH 16

THURSDAY, MARCH 17   *St. Patrick's Day*

FRIDAY, MARCH 18

SATURDAY, MARCH 19

Listen to my voice in the morning, LORD.
Each morning I bring my requests
to you and wait expectantly.
PSALM 5:3 NLT

Are you shy about praying in public? Don't be. Step out in faith, bow your head, and pray like God is the only One watching.

SUNDAY, MARCH 20   *First Day of Spring*

....

....

....

MONDAY, MARCH 21

....

....

....

TUESDAY, MARCH 22

....

....

....

WEDNESDAY, MARCH 23

THURSDAY, MARCH 24

FRIDAY, MARCH 25

SATURDAY, MARCH 26

So I bow in prayer before the Father from
whom every family in heaven and
on earth gets its true name.
EPHESIANS 3:14–15 NCV

Know that the Lord cares about every detail of your life, and nothing is a secret or a surprise to Him. Reach for the best, and expect results. You might have to wait for a time, but His answers are always unsurpassed.

SUNDAY, MARCH 27

MONDAY, MARCH 28

TUESDAY, MARCH 29

WEDNESDAY, MARCH 30

THURSDAY, MARCH 31

FRIDAY, APRIL 1

SATURDAY, APRIL 2

*Look to the L*ORD *and his*
strength; seek his face always.
PSALM 105:4 NIV

APRIL *2022*

SUNDAY	MONDAY	TUESDAY	WEDNESDAY
27	28	29	30
3	4	5	6
10 *Palm Sunday*	11	12	13
17 *Easter*	18	19	20
24	25	26	27

THURSDAY	FRIDAY	SATURDAY
31	1	2
7	8	9
14	15	16
	Passover Begins at Sundown / Good Friday	
21	22	23
28	29	30

MARCH

S	M	T	W	T	F	S
		1	2	3	4	5
6	7	8	9	10	11	12
13	14	15	16	17	18	19
20	21	22	23	24	25	26
27	28	29	30	31		

MAY

S	M	T	W	T	F	S
1	2	3	4	5	6	7
8	9	10	11	12	13	14
15	16	17	18	19	20	21
22	23	24	25	26	27	28
29	30	31				

THE POWER OF PRAYER

Have you given your heart to Jesus? If you have accepted Him as your Savior, you have taken on the *righteousness* of Christ. Certainly you are not perfect. In your humanity, you still sin and fall short. But God sees you through a Jesus lens! And so, your prayers reach the ears of your heavenly Father.

Pray often. Pray earnestly. Pray without ceasing. Pray about everything. Look at Jesus' example of prayer during His time on earth. He went away to quiet places such as gardens to pray. He prayed in solitude. He prayed with all His heart. If anyone was busy, it was the Messiah! But Jesus always made time to pray. We ought to follow His example. Prayer changes things.

---

*Lord, help me to believe in the power of prayer
and to make time for prayer daily. Amen.*

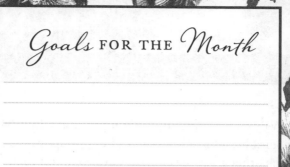

Goals FOR THE *Month*

....

....

....

....

....

....

....

....

....

....

....

....

*Confess your sins to each other and pray for each
other so that you may be healed. The earnest
prayer of a righteous person has great power
and produces wonderful results.*

JAMES 5:16 NLT

Waiting for a fresh outpouring of God's life-giving Spirit brings a newness and a fresh perspective on all the other areas of your life. Give your best each day by drawing on the strength of your heavenly Father.

SUNDAY, APRIL 3

MONDAY, APRIL 4

TUESDAY, APRIL 5

WEDNESDAY, APRIL 6

THURSDAY, APRIL 7

FRIDAY, APRIL 8

SATURDAY, APRIL 9

*But those who wait for the L*ORD *[who expect,
look for, and hope in Him] will gain new strength
and renew their power; they will lift up their
wings [and rise up close to God] like eagles.*
ISAIAH 40:31 AMP

What can you do when it seems the world is falling down around your shoulders? Stop. Take a deep breath, and then settle your mind on Jesus. Give Him the situation, the harried thoughts, the worries.

SUNDAY, APRIL 10 *Palm Sunday*

MONDAY, APRIL 11

TUESDAY, APRIL 12

WEDNESDAY, APRIL 13

THURSDAY, APRIL 14

FRIDAY, APRIL 15   *Passover Begins at Sundown /*
                                    Good Friday

SATURDAY, APRIL 16

*Do not be anxious about anything,
but in every situation, by prayer and petition,
with thanksgiving, present your requests to God.*
PHILIPPIANS 4:6 NIV

The Bible does not say to pray when it is convenient or as a last resort. It does not say to pray just in case prayer might work or to add prayer to a list of other things we are trying. We are instructed in Ephesians to pray at *all* times and on *every* occasion.

SUNDAY, APRIL 17 *Easter*

MONDAY, APRIL 18

TUESDAY, APRIL 19

WEDNESDAY, APRIL 20

THURSDAY, APRIL 21

FRIDAY, APRIL 22

SATURDAY, APRIL 23

Pray in the Spirit at all times and on every occasion.
Stay alert and be persistent in your prayers
for all believers everywhere.
EPHESIANS 6:18 NLT

Frustration and stress can keep us from clearly seeing the things that God puts before us. Time spent in prayer and meditation on God's Word can often wash away the dirt and grime of the day-to-day and provide a clear picture of God's intentions for our lives.

SUNDAY, APRIL 24

MONDAY, APRIL 25

TUESDAY, APRIL 26

WEDNESDAY, APRIL 27

THURSDAY, APRIL 28

FRIDAY, APRIL 29

SATURDAY, APRIL 30

Turning your ear to wisdom and applying your heart to understanding—indeed, if you call out for insight and cry aloud for understanding, and if you look for it as for silver and search for it as for hidden treasure, then you will understand the fear of the LORD and find the knowledge of God.

PROVERBS 2:2–5 NIV

MAY 2022

SUNDAY	MONDAY	TUESDAY	WEDNESDAY
1	2	3	4
8 *Mother's Day*	9	10	11
15	16	17	18
22	23	24	25
29	30 *Memorial Day*	31	1

THURSDAY	FRIDAY	SATURDAY
5	6	7
National Day of Prayer		
12	13	14
19	20	21
26	27	28
2	3	4

APRIL

S	M	T	W	T	F	S
					1	2
3	4	5	6	7	8	9
10	11	12	13	14	15	16
17	18	19	20	21	22	23
24	25	26	27	28	29	30

JUNE

S	M	T	W	T	F	S
			1	2	3	4
5	6	7	8	9	10	11
12	13	14	15	16	17	18
19	20	21	22	23	24	25
26	27	28	29	30		

PRAYER AND THE WORD UNLOCK THE DOOR

Math is a language all its own. Unfortunately, many students struggle to learn that language. Sometimes they never understand it completely but retain just enough of the language to make it through required courses.

Your spiritual life is also a different language. God's ways are not the ways of this world. Often His ways of doing things are similar to learning a new language. Prayer can unlock the door to understanding God's Word and His design for your life. As you spend time with God in prayer asking for understanding of His Word, His truth will speak to you in a brand-new way. The Holy Spirit will help you unlock the secrets of His purpose and plan for your life.

Heavenly Father, thank You for the Bible.
Help me to read it with understanding
and come to know You in a
whole new way. Amen.

Goals FOR THE *Month*

---

*I pray that your hearts will be flooded with light
so that you can understand the confident hope he
has given to those he called—his holy people
who are his rich and glorious inheritance.*

EPHESIANS 1:18 NLT

God targets every heart with the arrow of His Word.
It travels as far as the power of the One who thrust
it on its course. Prayer, coupled with God's Word
spoken to the unlovable, never misses the bull's-eye.

SUNDAY, MAY 1

MONDAY, MAY 2

TUESDAY, MAY 3

WEDNESDAY, MAY 4

THURSDAY, MAY 5   *National Day of Prayer*

FRIDAY, MAY 6

SATURDAY, MAY 7

Do nothing out of selfish ambition. . . .
Rather, in humility value others above yourselves,
not looking to your own interests but each of
you to the interests of the others.
PHILIPPIANS 2:3–4 NIV

Share your heart with God and gain His perspective on your troubles. The God who created you knows you better than anyone. Let Him be your first point of contact in any situation.

SUNDAY, MAY 8   *Mother's Day*

MONDAY, MAY 9

TUESDAY, MAY 10

WEDNESDAY, MAY 11

THURSDAY, MAY 12

FRIDAY, MAY 13

SATURDAY, MAY 14

Trust in him at all times, you people; pour out
your hearts to him, for God is our refuge.
PSALM 62:8 NIV

When we pray, rather than ask God why our prayers remain unanswered, perhaps we should ask the Lord to close our eyes so that we might see.

SUNDAY, MAY 15

....

....

....

MONDAY, MAY 16

....

....

....

TUESDAY, MAY 17

....

....

....

WEDNESDAY, MAY 18

THURSDAY, MAY 19

FRIDAY, MAY 20

SATURDAY, MAY 21

*"Therefore I tell you, whatever you ask
for in prayer, believe that you have
received it, and it will be yours."*
MARK 11:24 NIV

Do you have any difficulties in life, any burdens, worries, fears, relationship issues, finance troubles, or work problems that you need to "lay at the cross"? Jesus says, "Come."

SUNDAY, MAY 22

MONDAY, MAY 23

TUESDAY, MAY 24

WEDNESDAY, MAY 25

THURSDAY, MAY 26

FRIDAY, MAY 27

SATURDAY, MAY 28

*"Come to me, all you who are weary and burdened,
and I will give you rest. Take my yoke upon you and
learn from me. . .and you will find rest for your souls.
For my yoke is easy and my burden is light."*

Matthew 11:28–30 niv

JUNE *2022*

SUNDAY	MONDAY	TUESDAY	WEDNESDAY
29	30	31	1
5	6	7	8
12	13	14 *Flag Day*	15
19 *Father's Day*	20	21 *First Day of Summer*	22
26	27	28	29

THURSDAY	FRIDAY	SATURDAY
2	3	4
9	10	11
16	17	18
23	24	25
30	1	2

HOLY SPIRIT PRAYERS

Many times the burdens and troubles of our lives are too complicated to understand. It's difficult for us to put them into words, let alone know how to pray for what we need.

We can always take comfort in knowing that the Holy Spirit knows, understands, and pleads our case before the throne of God the Father. Our groans become words in the Holy Spirit's mouth, turning our mute prayers into praise and intercession "according to the will of God."

We can be encouraged, knowing that our deepest longings and desires, maybe unknown even to us, are presented before the God who knows us and loves us completely. Our names are engraved on His heart and hands. He never forgets us; He intervenes in all things for our good and His glory.

Father, I thank You for the encouragement these verses bring. May I always be aware of the Holy Spirit's interceding on my behalf. Amen.

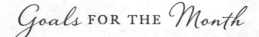

Goals FOR THE Month

....

....

....

....

....

....

....

....

....

....

*We do not know how to pray as we should,
but the Spirit Himself intercedes for us with
groanings too deep for words; and He who
searches the hearts knows what the mind of
the Spirit is, because He intercedes for the
saints according to the will of God.*

ROMANS 8:26–27 NASB

If we ask God to teach us how to pray, He will. It's all part of the prayer—ask God to lead you, then speak to Him from the heart.

SUNDAY, MAY 29

MONDAY, MAY 30   *Memorial Day*

TUESDAY, MAY 31

WEDNESDAY, JUNE 1

THURSDAY, JUNE 2

FRIDAY, JUNE 3

SATURDAY, JUNE 4

One of his disciples said to him, "Lord, teach us to pray, just as John taught his disciples." He said to them, "When you pray, say: 'Father, hallowed be your name, your kingdom come. Give us each day our daily bread.'"

LUKE 11:1–3 NIV

God likely has placed unbelievers in your life to whom He wants you to reach out. Share your faith with them in words and actions they can understand. Pray that the Lord opens their hearts to receive Jesus as Lord and Savior.

SUNDAY, JUNE 5

MONDAY, JUNE 6

TUESDAY, JUNE 7

WEDNESDAY, JUNE 8

THURSDAY, JUNE 9

FRIDAY, JUNE 10

SATURDAY, JUNE 11

*But people who aren't spiritual can't receive these truths
from God's Spirit. It all sounds foolish to them and
they can't understand it, for only those who are
spiritual can understand what the Spirit means.*

1 CORINTHIANS 2:14 NLT

Your prayers certainly don't have to be elaborate or polished. God does not judge your way with words. He knows your heart. He wants to hear from you.

SUNDAY, JUNE 12

MONDAY, JUNE 13

TUESDAY, JUNE 14   *Flag Day*

WEDNESDAY, JUNE 15

THURSDAY, JUNE 16

FRIDAY, JUNE 17

SATURDAY, JUNE 18

*"And when you are praying, do not use meaningless
repetition as the Gentiles do, for they suppose that
they will be heard for their many words."*
MATTHEW 6:7 NASB

JUNE 2022

God loves it when we witness for Him, live right, and instruct others in His Word. If those are things that we also truly desire, won't He grant us the "desires of our heart" and let us see people brought into the kingdom?

SUNDAY, JUNE 19   *Father's Day*

MONDAY, JUNE 20

TUESDAY, JUNE 21   *First Day of Summer*

WEDNESDAY, JUNE 22

THURSDAY, JUNE 23

FRIDAY, JUNE 24

SATURDAY, JUNE 25

Delight yourself in the LORD;
and He will give you the desires of your heart.
PSALM 37:4 NASB

Fortunately for us human beings, God isn't easily offended. He is deeply committed to holding up His end of our relationship, and He doesn't want us to hide anything from Him. He already knows every thought we have, anyway. Why not talk to Him about those thoughts?

SUNDAY, JUNE 26

MONDAY, JUNE 27

TUESDAY, JUNE 28

WEDNESDAY, JUNE 29

THURSDAY, JUNE 30

FRIDAY, JULY 1

SATURDAY, JULY 2

*"No one can come to Me unless the Father who sent
Me draws him [giving him the desire to
come to Me]; and I will raise him up
[from the dead] on the last day."*

JOHN 6:44 AMP

JULY 2022

SUNDAY	MONDAY	TUESDAY	WEDNESDAY
26	27	28	29
3	4 *Independence Day*	5	6
10	11	12	13
17	18	19	20
24 31	25	26	27

THURSDAY	FRIDAY	SATURDAY
30	1	2
7	8	9
14	15	16
21	22	23
28	29	30

JUNE

S	M	T	W	T	F	S
			1	2	3	4
5	6	7	8	9	10	11
12	13	14	15	16	17	18
19	20	21	22	23	24	25
26	27	28	29	30		

AUGUST

S	M	T	W	T	F	S
	1	2	3	4	5	6
7	8	9	10	11	12	13
14	15	16	17	18	19	20
21	22	23	24	25	26	27
28	29	30	31			

SUBMITTING TO GOD'S WILL

Many times submitting to God's will requires letting go of something we covet. We may be called to walk away from a relationship, a job, or a material possession. At other times, God may ask us to journey down a path we would not have chosen. Venturing out of our comfort zone or experiencing hardship is not our desire.

Embracing God's love enables us to submit to His will. God not only loves us immensely, but He desires to bless us abundantly. However, from our human perspective, those spiritual blessings may be disguised. That is why we must cling to truth. We must trust that God's ways are higher than ours. We must believe that His will is perfect. We must hold fast to His love. As we do, He imparts peace to our hearts, and we are able to say with conviction, "Your will be done."

Dear Lord, may I rest secure in Your unconditional love. Enable me to trust You more. May I desire that Your will be done in my life. Amen.

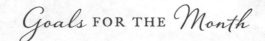

Goals FOR THE *Month*

"Your kingdom come, your will be done,
on earth as it is in heaven."
MATTHEW 6:10 NIV

If we let Him, God will replace the temporary supports we've relied on—health, independence, ability, you name it—with eternal spiritual supports like faith, surrender, and prayer. Those supports enable us to live a life of true freedom, one abounding with spiritual blessing.

SUNDAY, JULY 3

MONDAY, JULY 4   *Independence Day*

TUESDAY, JULY 5

WEDNESDAY, JULY 6

THURSDAY, JULY 7

FRIDAY, JULY 8

SATURDAY, JULY 9

God is the builder of everything.
HEBREWS 3:4 NIV

God will surround you with His love and protection—even if you're unconscious of His presence. He promises to keep our heads above water in life's storms.

SUNDAY, JULY 10

MONDAY, JULY 11

TUESDAY, JULY 12

WEDNESDAY, JULY 13

THURSDAY, JULY 14

FRIDAY, JULY 15

SATURDAY, JULY 16

My comfort in my suffering is this:
Your promise preserves my life.
PSALM 119:50 NIV

Often we allow the hectic pace of daily life to drain us physically and spiritually, and in the process, we deny ourselves time alone to pray and read God's Word. Meanwhile, God patiently waits.

SUNDAY, JULY 17

MONDAY, JULY 18

TUESDAY, JULY 19

WEDNESDAY, JULY 20

THURSDAY, JULY 21

FRIDAY, JULY 22

SATURDAY, JULY 23

*Then, because so many people were coming and
going that they did not even have a chance to eat,
he said to them, "Come with me by yourselves
to a quiet place and get some rest."*

MARK 6:31–32 NIV

Our world is filled with noise and distractions. Look for a place where you can be undisturbed for a few minutes. Take a deep breath, lift your prayers, and listen. God will speak—and your heart will hear.

SUNDAY, JULY 24

MONDAY, JULY 25

TUESDAY, JULY 26

WEDNESDAY, JULY 27

THURSDAY, JULY 28

FRIDAY, JULY 29

SATURDAY, JULY 30

*"And I will ask the Father, and He will give
you another Helper (Comforter, Advocate,
Intercessor—Counselor, Strengthener,
Standby), to be with you forever."*
JOHN 14:16 AMP

AUGUST *2022*

SUNDAY	MONDAY	TUESDAY	WEDNESDAY
31	1	2	3
7	8	9	10
14	15	16	17
21	22	23	24
28	29	30	31

THURSDAY	FRIDAY	SATURDAY
4	5	6
11	12	13
18	19	20
25	26	27
1	2	3

JULY

S	M	T	W	T	F	S
					1	2
3	4	5	6	7	8	9
10	11	12	13	14	15	16
17	18	19	20	21	22	23
24	25	26	27	28	29	30
31						

SEPTEMBER

S	M	T	W	T	F	S
				1	2	3
4	5	6	7	8	9	10
11	12	13	14	15	16	17
18	19	20	21	22	23	24
25	26	27	28	29	30	

WHAT IS YOUR REQUEST?

Be patient. What we may view as a non-answer may simply be God saying, "Wait" or "I have something better for you." He *will* answer. Keep in mind that His ways are not our ways, nor are His thoughts our thoughts.

God knows what He's doing, even when He allows trials in our lives. We might think that saving a loved one from difficulty is a great idea—but God, in His wisdom, may decide that would be keeping them (or us) from an opportunity for spiritual growth. Since we don't know all of God's plans, we must simply lay our requests before Him and trust Him to do what is right. He will never fail us!

Father God, here are my needs.
I lay them at Your feet, walking away
unburdened and assured that You have
everything under control. Thank You! Amen.

Goals FOR THE Month

And pray in the Spirit on all occasions with
all kinds of prayers and requests. With this in
mind, be alert and always keep on praying.

EPHESIANS 6:18 NIV

Praise chases away the doldrums and tips our lips up in a smile. With a renewed spirit of optimism and hope, we can thank the Giver of all things good.

SUNDAY, JULY 31

MONDAY, AUGUST 1

TUESDAY, AUGUST 2

WEDNESDAY, AUGUST 3

THURSDAY, AUGUST 4

FRIDAY, AUGUST 5

SATURDAY, AUGUST 6

*He restoreth my soul: he leadeth me in the
paths of righteousness for his name's sake.*
PSALM 23:3 KJV

When we come to the end of our rope, God ties a knot. And God will do great things in and through us, if we will just hold on.

SUNDAY, AUGUST 7

MONDAY, AUGUST 8

TUESDAY, AUGUST 9

WEDNESDAY, AUGUST 10

THURSDAY, AUGUST 11

FRIDAY, AUGUST 12

SATURDAY, AUGUST 13

Let us not become weary in doing good,
for at the proper time we will reap
a harvest if we do not give up.
GALATIANS 6:9 NIV

When we release our cares to the Lord in prayer, His peace washes over us and fills our hearts and minds. What a comfort is the peace of God when we find ourselves in the valley.

SUNDAY, AUGUST 14

MONDAY, AUGUST 15

TUESDAY, AUGUST 16

WEDNESDAY, AUGUST 17

THURSDAY, AUGUST 18

FRIDAY, AUGUST 19

SATURDAY, AUGUST 20

*Be anxious for nothing, but in everything by prayer
and supplication, with thanksgiving, let your requests
be made known to God; and the peace of God,
which surpasses all understanding, will guard
your hearts and minds through Christ Jesus.*

PHILIPPIANS 4:6–7 NKJV

AUGUST 2022

It is often in the stillness of our lives that we hear God best. When we take time to think, meditate on scripture, pray, and reflect, we find that we can indeed hear His still, small voice.

SUNDAY, AUGUST 21

MONDAY, AUGUST 22

TUESDAY, AUGUST 23

WEDNESDAY, AUGUST 24

THURSDAY, AUGUST 25

FRIDAY, AUGUST 26

SATURDAY, AUGUST 27

*He was oppressed, and he was afflicted, yet he
opened not his mouth; like a lamb that is led
to the slaughter, and like a sheep that before its
shearers is silent, so he opened not his mouth.*
ISAIAH 53:7 ESV

The Bible instructs us to live by faith—not by feelings. Faith assures us that daylight will dawn in our darkest moments, affirming God's presence so that even when we fail to pray and positive feelings fade, our moods surrender to song.

SUNDAY, AUGUST 28

MONDAY, AUGUST 29

TUESDAY, AUGUST 30

WEDNESDAY, AUGUST 31

THURSDAY, SEPTEMBER 1

FRIDAY, SEPTEMBER 2

SATURDAY, SEPTEMBER 3

*No man is justified by the law in the sight of God,
it is evident: for, The just shall live by faith.*

GALATIANS 3:11 KJV

SEPTEMBER *2022*

SUNDAY	MONDAY	TUESDAY	WEDNESDAY
28	29	30	31
4	5 *Labor Day*	6	7
11	12	13	14
18	19	20	21
25	26	27	28

THURSDAY	FRIDAY	SATURDAY
1	2	3
8	9	10
15	16	17
22	23	24
29 *First Day of Autumn*	30	1

AUGUST

S	M	T	W	T	F	S
	1	2	3	4	5	6
7	8	9	10	11	12	13
14	15	16	17	18	19	20
21	22	23	24	25	26	27
28	29	30	31			

OCTOBER

S	M	T	W	T	F	S
						1
2	3	4	5	6	7	8
9	10	11	12	13	14	15
16	17	18	19	20	21	22
23	24	25	26	27	28	29
30	31					

FOLLOW THE LORD'S FOOTSTEPS

Jesus asked His disciples to follow Him, and He asks us to do the same. It sounds simple, but following Jesus can be a challenge. Sometimes we become impatient, not wanting to wait upon the Lord. We run ahead of Him by taking matters into our own hands and making decisions without consulting Him first. Or perhaps we aren't diligent to keep in step with Him. We fall behind, and soon Jesus seems so far away.

Following Jesus requires staying right on His heels. We need to be close enough to hear His whisper. Stay close to His heart by opening the Bible daily. Allow His Word to speak to your heart and give you direction. Throughout the day, offer up prayers for guidance and wisdom. Keep in step with Him, and His close presence will bless you beyond measure.

Dear Lord, grant me the desire to follow You. Help me not to run ahead or lag behind. Amen.

Goals FOR THE Month

_____

_____

_____

_____

_____

_____

_____

_____

_____

_____

_____

_____

_____

"Come, follow me," Jesus said,
"and I will send you out to fish for people."
MATTHEW 4:19 NIV

When we seek our heavenly Father before daily activities demand our attention, the Holy Spirit regenerates our spirits, and our cups overflow.

SUNDAY, SEPTEMBER 4

MONDAY, SEPTEMBER 5　　　　　　　　　*Labor Day*

TUESDAY, SEPTEMBER 6

WEDNESDAY, SEPTEMBER 7

THURSDAY, SEPTEMBER 8

FRIDAY, SEPTEMBER 9

SATURDAY, SEPTEMBER 10

O God, thou art my God;
early will I seek thee.
PSALM 63:1 KJV

Whatever you face, wherever you go, whatever dreams you have for your life, take courage and know that anything is possible when you draw on the power of God.

SUNDAY, SEPTEMBER 11

MONDAY, SEPTEMBER 12

TUESDAY, SEPTEMBER 13

WEDNESDAY, SEPTEMBER 14

THURSDAY, SEPTEMBER 15

FRIDAY, SEPTEMBER 16

SATURDAY, SEPTEMBER 17

*The Spirit of God, who raised
Jesus from the dead, lives in you.*
ROMANS 8:11 NLT

Do you yearn for a place where problems evaporate like the morning dew? Do you need a place of solace? God is wherever you are—behind a bedroom door, in your favorite chair, or even at a sink full of dirty dishes. Come apart and enter God's mountain sanctuary.

SUNDAY, SEPTEMBER 18

MONDAY, SEPTEMBER 19

TUESDAY, SEPTEMBER 20

WEDNESDAY, SEPTEMBER 21

THURSDAY, SEPTEMBER 22   *First Day of Autumn*

FRIDAY, SEPTEMBER 23

SATURDAY, SEPTEMBER 24

*And seeing the multitudes, he went up into a
mountain. . .and. . .his disciples came unto him:
and he opened his mouth, and taught them.*

MATTHEW 5:1–2 KJV

Don't delay. Take time right when you receive a request to talk to the Lord on the requester's behalf. Be the bridge that carries that person through the valley of darkness back to the mountaintop of joy.

SUNDAY, SEPTEMBER 25

MONDAY, SEPTEMBER 26

TUESDAY, SEPTEMBER 27

WEDNESDAY, SEPTEMBER 28

THURSDAY, SEPTEMBER 29

FRIDAY, SEPTEMBER 30

SATURDAY, OCTOBER 1

*"I looked for someone among them who would build
up the wall and stand before me in the gap on
behalf of the land so I would not have to
destroy it, but I found no one."*

EZEKIEL 22:30 NIV

OCTOBER 2022

SUNDAY	MONDAY	TUESDAY	WEDNESDAY
25	26	27	28
2	3	4	5
9	10	11	12
	Columbus Day		
16	17	18	19
23	24	25	26
	Halloween		
30	31		

THURSDAY	FRIDAY	SATURDAY
29	30	1
6	7	8
13	14	15
20	21	22
27	28	29

OCT

SEPTEMBER

S	M	T	W	T	F	S
				1	2	3
4	5	6	7	8	9	10
11	12	13	14	15	16	17
18	19	20	21	22	23	24
25	26	27	28	29	30	

NOVEMBER

S	M	T	W	T	F	S
		1	2	3	4	5
6	7	8	9	10	11	12
13	14	15	16	17	18	19
20	21	22	23	24	25	26
27	28	29	30			

PERFECT PRAYERS

How many times have we made prayer a mere religious exercise, performed best by the "holy elite," rather than what it really is—conversation with God our Father?

Just pour out your heart to God. Share how your day went. Tell Him your dreams. Ask Him to search you and reveal areas of compromise. Thank Him for your lunch. Plead for your family and friends' well-being. Complain about your car. . . . Just talk with Him. Don't worry about how impressive (or unimpressive!) you sound.

Talk with God while doing dishes, driving the car, folding laundry, eating lunch, or kneeling by your bed. Whenever, wherever, whatever—tell Him. He cares!

Don't allow this day to slip away without talking to your Father. No perfection required.

Father God, what a privilege it is to unburden my heart to You. Teach me the beauty and simplicity of simply sharing my day with You. Amen.

Goals FOR THE *Month*

"Pray, then, in this way: 'Our Father. . .'"
Out of the depths [of distress] I
have cried to You, O LORD.

MATTHEW 6:9 AMP; PSALM 130:1 AMP

When was the last time you did an anxiety check? Days? Weeks? Months? Chances are, you're due for another. After all, we're instructed not to be anxious about anything. Instead, we're to present our requests to God with thanksgiving in our hearts. We're to turn to Him in prayer so that He can take our burdens.

SUNDAY, OCTOBER 2

MONDAY, OCTOBER 3

TUESDAY, OCTOBER 4

WEDNESDAY, OCTOBER 5

THURSDAY, OCTOBER 6

FRIDAY, OCTOBER 7

SATURDAY, OCTOBER 8

Do not be anxious about anything,
but in every situation, by prayer and petition,
with thanksgiving, present your requests to God.
PHILIPPIANS 4:6 NIV

Prayer is an act of worship on the part of the created toward the Creator. Prayer is simply "talking to God" about everything that affects our lives.

SUNDAY, OCTOBER 9

MONDAY, OCTOBER 10   *Columbus Day*

TUESDAY, OCTOBER 11

WEDNESDAY, OCTOBER 12

THURSDAY, OCTOBER 13

FRIDAY, OCTOBER 14

SATURDAY, OCTOBER 15

*First of all, then, I urge that entreaties and prayers,
petitions and thanksgivings, be made on behalf of
all men, for kings and all who are in authority,
so that we may lead a tranquil and quiet
life in all godliness and dignity.*

1 TIMOTHY 2:1–2 NASB

OCTOBER 2022

Consider the dawning of the day as an opportunity to begin anew with our heavenly Father. Seek Him in the morning through studying His Word and through prayer, embracing His compassion to be a blessing to others throughout your day.

SUNDAY, OCTOBER 16

MONDAY, OCTOBER 17

TUESDAY, OCTOBER 18

WEDNESDAY, OCTOBER 19

THURSDAY, OCTOBER 20

FRIDAY, OCTOBER 21

SATURDAY, OCTOBER 22

Because of the Lord's great love we are not consumed,
for his compassions never fail. They are new every
morning; great is your faithfulness.
LAMENTATIONS 3:22–23 NIV

Be quick to confess sin in order to run the race unhindered. Persevere. Jesus waits at the finish line. The reward will be well worth it!

SUNDAY, OCTOBER 23

MONDAY, OCTOBER 24

TUESDAY, OCTOBER 25

WEDNESDAY, OCTOBER 26

THURSDAY, OCTOBER 27

FRIDAY, OCTOBER 28

SATURDAY, OCTOBER 29

Therefore, since we are surrounded by such a great cloud of witnesses, let us throw off everything that hinders and the sin that so easily entangles. And let us run with perseverance the race marked out for us.

HEBREWS 12:1 NIV

NOVEMBER  2022

SUNDAY	MONDAY	TUESDAY	WEDNESDAY
30	31	1	2
6 *Daylight Saving Time Ends*	7	8 *Election Day*	9
13	14	15	16
20	21	22	23
27	28	29	30

THURSDAY	FRIDAY	SATURDAY
3	4	5
10	11	12
	Veterans Day	
17	18	19
24	25	26
Thanksgiving Day		
1	2	3

OCTOBER

S	M	T	W	T	F	S
						1
2	3	4	5	6	7	8
9	10	11	12	13	14	15
16	17	18	19	20	21	22
23	24	25	26	27	28	29
30	31					

DECEMBER

S	M	T	W	T	F	S
				1	2	3
4	5	6	7	8	9	10
11	12	13	14	15	16	17
18	19	20	21	22	23	24
25	26	27	28	29	30	31

LEARNING AS WE GROW

When King David died, Solomon became the king of Israel. Just like a child who does not yet know how to put away his toys, Solomon confessed that he did not know how to carry out his duties as king of Israel. Instead of sitting down on his throne in despair, though, Solomon called on the name of the Lord for help.

As Christians, we are sometimes like little children. We know what our duties as Christians are, but we do not know how to carry them out. Just like Solomon, we can ask God for help and guidance in the completion of our responsibilities. God hears our prayers and is faithful in teaching us our duties, just as He was faithful to Solomon in teaching him his.

Dear Lord, thank You for being willing to teach me my Christian responsibilities. Help me to learn willingly and eagerly. Amen.

Goals FOR THE Month

"But I am only a little child and do not know how to carry out my duties."
1 KINGS 3:7 NIV

Daily and hourly, we can pray for Christ's leading, asking Him to keep us focused on Him and mindful that we are following Him. He has a path that He desires to walk with each of us, guiding us each step of the way.

SUNDAY, OCTOBER 30

MONDAY, OCTOBER 31   *Halloween*

TUESDAY, NOVEMBER 1

WEDNESDAY, NOVEMBER 2

THURSDAY, NOVEMBER 3

FRIDAY, NOVEMBER 4

SATURDAY, NOVEMBER 5

*Lead me, LORD, in your righteousness because of
my enemies—make your way straight before me.*
PSALM 5:8 NIV

Even in our worst situations, we need to approach God with both repentance and thanksgiving. No matter our experiences, we serve a powerful God— One who deserves all honor and praise.

SUNDAY, NOVEMBER 6   *Daylight Saving Time Ends*

MONDAY, NOVEMBER 7

TUESDAY, NOVEMBER 8   *Election Day*

WEDNESDAY, NOVEMBER 9

THURSDAY, NOVEMBER 10

FRIDAY, NOVEMBER 11   *Veterans Day*

SATURDAY, NOVEMBER 12

*"In my distress I called to the L*ORD*,
and he answered me. From deep in the
realm of the dead I called for help,
and you listened to my cry."*

JONAH 2:2 NIV

When we trust in God, those around us will see His power in us. Through our actions, others will come to know God and proclaim that He is a God of gods and a Lord of kings.

SUNDAY, NOVEMBER 13

MONDAY, NOVEMBER 14

TUESDAY, NOVEMBER 15

WEDNESDAY, NOVEMBER 16

THURSDAY, NOVEMBER 17

FRIDAY, NOVEMBER 18

SATURDAY, NOVEMBER 19

*"Surely your God is a God of gods and a Lord of
kings and a revealer of mysteries, since you
have been able to reveal this mystery."*

DANIEL 2:47 NASB

Go to God in prayer. Seek answers from His Word and from the Holy Spirit. He will do a great work in your life. He will be faithful to complete what He started in you—and you will become like Him.

SUNDAY, NOVEMBER 20

MONDAY, NOVEMBER 21

TUESDAY, NOVEMBER 22

WEDNESDAY, NOVEMBER 23

THURSDAY, NOVEMBER 24   *Thanksgiving Day*

FRIDAY, NOVEMBER 25

SATURDAY, NOVEMBER 26

Being confident of this very thing, that he which
hath begun a good work in you will perform
it until the day of Jesus Christ.
PHILIPPIANS 1:6 KJV

Praying for Christians everywhere requires us to engage in a world we might not always be involved with, but God wants us to love and pray for our Christian family whether they are around the corner or around the world.

SUNDAY, NOVEMBER 27

MONDAY, NOVEMBER 28

TUESDAY, NOVEMBER 29

WEDNESDAY, NOVEMBER 30

THURSDAY, DECEMBER 1

FRIDAY, DECEMBER 2

SATURDAY, DECEMBER 3

Pray in the Spirit at all times and on every occasion.
Stay alert and be persistent in your prayers
for all believers everywhere.
EPHESIANS 6:18 NLT

DECEMBER *2022*

SUNDAY	MONDAY	TUESDAY	WEDNESDAY
27	28	29	30
4	5	6	7
11	12	13	14
18	19	20	21
Hanukkah Begins at Sundown			*First Day of Winter*
25	26	27	28
Christmas Day			

THURSDAY	FRIDAY	SATURDAY
1	2	3
8	9	10
15	16	17
22	23	24 *Christmas Eve*
29	30	31 *New Year's Eve*

NOVEMBER

S	M	T	W	T	F	S
		1	2	3	4	5
6	7	8	9	10	11	12
13	14	15	16	17	18	19
20	21	22	23	24	25	26
27	28	29	30			

JANUARY

S	M	T	W	T	F	S
1	2	3	4	5	6	7
8	9	10	11	12	13	14
15	16	17	18	19	20	21
22	23	24	25	26	27	28
29	30	31				

PRAYING FOR LOVED ONES

One of the best things a woman can do for her loved ones is pray for them. And while we don't find one simple formula for effective prayer in the Bible, *how* we pray may be just as important as *what* we pray.

Do we beseech God with faith, believing that He can do anything? Or do we pray with hesitation, believing that nothing is going to change? God is honored and willing to work when we pray with faith.

The most beneficial times of prayer often come when we make time to listen to God, not just talk "at" Him. He can give us wisdom and insights we would never come up with on our own.

Though we can't always see it, God is at work in our loved ones' hearts and in ours.

Lord, thank You for Your concern for my friends and family members. I know You love them even more than I do. Amen.

Goals FOR THE Month

----

*"Therefore I tell you, whatever you ask
for in prayer, believe that you have
received it, and it will be yours."*

MARK 11:24 NIV

Ask the Lord to help you develop a true reverence for Him. He wants us to call Him *Abba* Father ("Daddy"), but He also demands respect, reverence, and a holy fear. He is the God of the universe—the same yesterday, today, and tomorrow.

SUNDAY, DECEMBER 4

MONDAY, DECEMBER 5

TUESDAY, DECEMBER 6

WEDNESDAY, DECEMBER 7

THURSDAY, DECEMBER 8

FRIDAY, DECEMBER 9

SATURDAY, DECEMBER 10

Charm is deceptive, and beauty is fleeting;
but a woman who fears the LORD is to be praised.
Honor her for all that her hands have done,
and let her works bring her praise at the city gate.
PROVERBS 31:30–31 NIV

The Spirit knows our subtle moods, our heartaches, and our soul cravings. We must turn to Him in transparent prayer, mulling the Word over in our minds, allowing it to penetrate the hidden recesses of our souls.

SUNDAY, DECEMBER 11

MONDAY, DECEMBER 12

TUESDAY, DECEMBER 13

WEDNESDAY, DECEMBER 14

THURSDAY, DECEMBER 15

FRIDAY, DECEMBER 16

SATURDAY, DECEMBER 17

*As the deer pants for streams of water, so
my soul pants for you, my God. My soul
thirsts for God, for the living God.
When can I go and meet with God?*

PSALM 42:1–2 NIV

If you realize your weakness and acknowledge your need, then prayer will become vital to your existence. It will become your sustenance and nourishment—your lifeline. Prayer reveals your dependence upon God. How much do you need Him?

SUNDAY, DECEMBER 18 *Hanukkah Begins at Sundown*

MONDAY, DECEMBER 19

TUESDAY, DECEMBER 20

WEDNESDAY, DECEMBER 21   *First Day of Winter*

THURSDAY, DECEMBER 22

FRIDAY, DECEMBER 23

SATURDAY, DECEMBER 24   *Christmas Eve*

*Then Jesus went with his disciples to a place
called Gethsemane, and he said to them,
"Sit here while I go over there and pray."*
MATTHEW 26:36 NIV

DECEMBER 2022

Make a list of the blessings in your life and thank the Provider of those blessings. Choose not to focus on yourself; instead, praise Him for being Him. Soon you'll feel true, holy refreshment—the freedom God wants you to live out every day.

SUNDAY, DECEMBER 25   *Christmas Day*

MONDAY, DECEMBER 26

TUESDAY, DECEMBER 27

WEDNESDAY, DECEMBER 28

THURSDAY, DECEMBER 29

FRIDAY, DECEMBER 30

SATURDAY, DECEMBER 31   *New Year's Eve*

*Why, my soul, are you downcast? Why so disturbed
within me? Put your hope in God, for I will yet
praise him, my Savior and my God.*
PSALM 42:11 NIV

NOTES:

NOTES:

NOTES:

NOTES:

NOTES:

NOTES:

CONTACTS

Name:

Address:

Phone: Cell:

Email:

Name:

Address:

Phone: Cell:

Email:

Name:

Address:

Phone: Cell:

Email:

Name:

Address:

Phone: Cell:

Email:

CONTACTS

Name:

Address:

Phone: Cell:

Email:

Name:

Address:

Phone: Cell:

Email:

Name:

Address:

Phone: Cell:

Email:

Name:

Address:

Phone: Cell:

Email:

CONTACTS

Name:

Address:

Phone: Cell:

Email:

Name:

Address:

Phone: Cell:

Email:

Name:

Address:

Phone: Cell:

Email:

Name:

Address:

Phone: Cell:

Email:

CONTACTS

Name:

Address:

Phone: Cell:

Email:

Name:

Address:

Phone: Cell:

Email:

Name:

Address:

Phone: Cell:

Email:

Name:

Address:

Phone: Cell:

Email:

CONTACTS

Name:

Address:

Phone: Cell:

Email:

Name:

Address:

Phone: Cell:

Email:

Name:

Address:

Phone: Cell:

Email:

Name:

Address:

Phone: Cell:

Email:

CONTACTS

Name:

Address:

Phone: Cell:

Email:

Name:

Address:

Phone: Cell:

Email:

Name:

Address:

Phone: Cell:

Email:

Name:

Address:

Phone: Cell:

Email:

CONTACTS

Name:

Address:

Phone: Cell:

Email:

Name:

Address:

Phone: Cell:

Email:

Name:

Address:

Phone: Cell:

Email:

Name:

Address:

Phone: Cell:

Email:

CONTACTS

Name:

Address:

Phone: Cell:

Email:

Name:

Address:

Phone: Cell:

Email:

Name:

Address:

Phone: Cell:

Email:

Name:

Address:

Phone: Cell:

Email:

CONTACTS

Name:

Address:

Phone: Cell:

Email:

Name:

Address:

Phone: Cell:

Email:

Name:

Address:

Phone: Cell:

Email:

Name:

Address:

Phone: Cell:

Email:

CONTACTS

Name:

Address:

Phone: Cell:

Email:

Name:

Address:

Phone: Cell:

Email:

Name:

Address:

Phone: Cell:

Email:

Name:

Address:

Phone: Cell:

Email:

2023

JANUARY

S	M	T	W	T	F	S
1	2	3	4	5	6	7
8	9	10	11	12	13	14
15	16	17	18	19	20	21
22	23	24	25	26	27	28
29	30	31				

FEBRUARY

S	M	T	W	T	F	S
			1	2	3	4
5	6	7	8	9	10	11
12	13	14	15	16	17	18
19	20	21	22	23	24	25
26	27	28				

MARCH

S	M	T	W	T	F	S
			1	2	3	4
5	6	7	8	9	10	11
12	13	14	15	16	17	18
19	20	21	22	23	24	25
26	27	28	29	30	31	

APRIL

S	M	T	W	T	F	S
						1
2	3	4	5	6	7	8
9	10	11	12	13	14	15
16	17	18	19	20	21	22
23	24	25	26	27	28	29
30						

MAY

S	M	T	W	T	F	S
	1	2	3	4	5	6
7	8	9	10	11	12	13
14	15	16	17	18	19	20
21	22	23	24	25	26	27
28	29	30	31			

JUNE

S	M	T	W	T	F	S
				1	2	3
4	5	6	7	8	9	10
11	12	13	14	15	16	17
18	19	20	21	22	23	24
25	26	27	28	29	30	

JULY

S	M	T	W	T	F	S
						1
2	3	4	5	6	7	8
9	10	11	12	13	14	15
16	17	18	19	20	21	22
23	24	25	26	27	28	29
30	31					

AUGUST

S	M	T	W	T	F	S
		1	2	3	4	5
6	7	8	9	10	11	12
13	14	15	16	17	18	19
20	21	22	23	24	25	26
27	28	29	30	31		

SEPTEMBER

S	M	T	W	T	F	S
					1	2
3	4	5	6	7	8	9
10	11	12	13	14	15	16
17	18	19	20	21	22	23
24	25	26	27	28	29	30

OCTOBER

S	M	T	W	T	F	S
1	2	3	4	5	6	7
8	9	10	11	12	13	14
15	16	17	18	19	20	21
22	23	24	25	26	27	28
29	30	31				

NOVEMBER

S	M	T	W	T	F	S
			1	2	3	4
5	6	7	8	9	10	11
12	13	14	15	16	17	18
19	20	21	22	23	24	25
26	27	28	29	30		

DECEMBER

S	M	T	W	T	F	S
					1	2
3	4	5	6	7	8	9
10	11	12	13	14	15	16
17	18	19	20	21	22	23
24	25	26	27	28	29	30
31						

2024

JANUARY

S	M	T	W	T	F	S
	1	2	3	4	5	6
7	8	9	10	11	12	13
14	15	16	17	18	19	20
21	22	23	24	25	26	27
28	29	30	31			

FEBRUARY

S	M	T	W	T	F	S
				1	2	3
4	5	6	7	8	9	10
11	12	13	14	15	16	17
18	19	20	21	22	23	24
25	26	27	28	29		

MARCH

S	M	T	W	T	F	S
					1	2
3	4	5	6	7	8	9
10	11	12	13	14	15	16
17	18	19	20	21	22	23
24	25	26	27	28	29	30
31						

APRIL

S	M	T	W	T	F	S
	1	2	3	4	5	6
7	8	9	10	11	12	13
14	15	16	17	18	19	20
21	22	23	24	25	26	27
28	29	30				

MAY

S	M	T	W	T	F	S
			1	2	3	4
5	6	7	8	9	10	11
12	13	14	15	16	17	18
19	20	21	22	23	24	25
26	27	28	29	30	31	

JUNE

S	M	T	W	T	F	S
						1
2	3	4	5	6	7	8
9	10	11	12	13	14	15
16	17	18	19	20	21	22
23	24	25	26	27	28	29
30						

JULY

S	M	T	W	T	F	S
	1	2	3	4	5	6
7	8	9	10	11	12	13
14	15	16	17	18	19	20
21	22	23	24	25	26	27
28	29	30	31			

AUGUST

S	M	T	W	T	F	S
				1	2	3
4	5	6	7	8	9	10
11	12	13	14	15	16	17
18	19	20	21	22	23	24
25	26	27	28	29	30	31

SEPTEMBER

S	M	T	W	T	F	S
1	2	3	4	5	6	7
8	9	10	11	12	13	14
15	16	17	18	19	20	21
22	23	24	25	26	27	28
29	30					

OCTOBER

S	M	T	W	T	F	S
		1	2	3	4	5
6	7	8	9	10	11	12
13	14	15	16	17	18	19
20	21	22	23	24	25	26
27	28	29	30	31		

NOVEMBER

S	M	T	W	T	F	S
					1	2
3	4	5	6	7	8	9
10	11	12	13	14	15	16
17	18	19	20	21	22	23
24	25	26	27	28	29	30

DECEMBER

S	M	T	W	T	F	S
1	2	3	4	5	6	7
8	9	10	11	12	13	14
15	16	17	18	19	20	21
22	23	24	25	26	27	28
29	30	31				